THE NEW AMERICAN CONTINENT

THE NEW AMERICAN CONTINENT
Our Continental Shelf

Norman Carlisle

J. B. LIPPINCOTT COMPANY
New York and Philadelphia

ALSO BY NORMAN CARLISLE

SATELLITES: Servants of Man

The author is grateful to the following for the photographs in this book: Armco Steel and the Marine Technology Society, 66, 91; Ball Brothers Research, 21 (upper); California Dept. of Fish and Game, 44, 45, 46 (upper), 46 (lower); California Institute of Technology, 33 (lower); Chemetron, Inc., 67 (upper); Deep Sea Ventures, Inc., 57; Duke University, 17, 19 (upper), 19 (lower), 22, 24, 55, 72; duPont, 75; EG&G, 20; Edo Western Corp., 21 (lower); Environmental Protection Agency, 32; Exxon, 30, 58; Florida Dept. of Natural Resources, 13 (lower); Florida State News Bureau, 81; Florida State University, 33 (upper); Freeport Minerals Co., 59; General Dynamics, 56, 65 (lower), 71 (lower), 92; General Electric, 64, 88, 89, 90; Leslie Salt Co., 62; Makai Company, 86; Marine Research Laboratory, Florida Dept. of Natural Resources, 35; Marine Science Center, Oregon State University, 34; Mobil Oil Corp., 26, 28, 60; NASA, 2, 87; National Marine Fisheries Service, 41, 42, 43, 48, 52, 82 (upper), 82 (lower); National Park Service, 8, 40, 77, 83; National Research Council of Canada, 50 (upper), 50 (lower), 51; Natural Resources Institute, University of Maryland, 23 (upper), 36, 49; Oak Ridge National Laboratory, 63; Ocean Systems, Inc., 15; Perry Oceanographics, 16; Perry Submarine Builders, 14; Reynolds Metals Corp., 71 (upper); *Science and Children*, 10 (upper); Shell Oil Company, 13 (upper), 26, 27, 79; Socony Vacuum Oil Co., 80; Standard Oil of California, 37; Stanford University, 10 (lower), 53; Unisuit U.S.A., 12 (lower); U.S. Atomic Energy Commission, 31; U.S. Bureau of Reclamation, 74; U.S. Coast Guard, 38 (upper), 38 (lower), 39; U.S. Geological Survey, 23 (lower), 54; U.S. Navy, 11, 12 (upper), 18, 25, 65 (upper), 67 (lower), 68, 69, 70, 73, 84, 85; University of California, San Diego, 78; University of Connecticut, 29, 47, 61; Virginia Dept. of Conservation, 76.

U.S. Library of Congress Cataloging in Publication Data

Carlisle, Norman V   birth date
   The new American Continent: our continental shelf.

   SUMMARY: Describes the American continental shelf and the research conducted to discover more about it.
   Bibliography: p.
1. Continental shelf—United States—Juvenile literature. [1. Continental shelf]
   I. Title.
   GC85.2.U6C37   551.4'1   72-13422
   ISBN-0-397-31234-2

CONTENTS

FOREWORD

"It's a whole new American continent!"

These were the words of a great oceanographer who had long ranged the world's wide seas—the late Columbus O'Donnell Iselin of Woods Hole Oceanographic Institution. He was talking to me about the wondrous region that few people think of as being part of our country—the continental shelf.

I don't know whether Dr. Iselin coined the phrase, but I do know that it is an apt one to use in describing the vast submerged terrace that borders our land continent.

Just what *is* the continental shelf?

By international agreement, it is defined as the land extending out from the shore to a point where the water depth reaches 200 meters, or 656 feet. There is considerable variation in its width. Off the United States, the shelf is a narrow 10 miles wide at some points off California, 175 miles wide off Cape Cod, 300 miles wide off Alaska. In 1958, the International Convention of the Continental Shelf declared that every coastal country had legal rights to the shelf off its shores. This, in effect, added about 850,000 square miles of land to the United States—the largest acquisition of land since the Louisiana Purchase of 1803, which included about 825,000 square miles.

This vast land and the waters above it offer us many riches. They can provide us with a new abundance of food; replenish our dwindling supplies of minerals, oil, and natural gas; and increasingly become a fascinating playground for millions.

Will we make wise use of this rich new domain? Will we be able to protect it from the menace of pollution? Will we do better by this new underwater frontier than we have by the dry land of our familiar "old continent"? Let us hope that in exploiting it we do not damage it, that in enjoying it we do not ravage it, that our future will be enriched by our pioneering ventures onto the "new American continent."

1 · EXPLORING THE CONTINENTAL SHELF

"The present imperfect state of knowledge of our offshore regions," says a report of the U.S. Geological Survey, "is comparable to what was known of the western states and Territories during the mid 1800s."

Here, indeed, is a continent waiting to be explored. Not only are the adventurous pioneers of the underwater world faced with learning about the *square* miles of its land area, they must concern themselves equally with the millions of *cubic* miles of water that lie above the plains, the hills, the canyons of this new American continent.

Exploration of the continental shelf begins on the fringe of land that is briefly revealed when the restless tide recedes. Although it is constantly being explored and studied by professional scientists, this seaside zone is also a province open to amateurs—as these children in New Jersey and these Stanford University students in California are happily demonstrating.

To really explore the continental shelf, scientists must go into the water that covers it. Geologists, marine biologists, oceanographers and engineers make tens of thousands of dives each year. They are the pathfinders who are opening up the new land beneath the sea.

The searches of the scientific divers extend from the Arctic, where the sea is roofed with ice and the shelf itself stony and barren . . .

. . . to the semitropical waters off Florida, where warm water diving is easy and the surface of the shelf rich in sea life.

Exploration of the continental shelf is being speeded by a new breed of submersibles—small, agile craft that can move swiftly at any desired depth or hover in one spot. Observation through portholes is aided by powerful lights that can push back the darkness at depths sunlight does not penetrate. Mechanical arms operated from inside can pick up specimens of soil, rocks, and marine growth. Many of the new submersibles are made for deep ocean work, but some, like the *Shelf Diver*, are designed for the specific purpose of working in the waters above the shelf.

Some of the shelf-exploring submarines permit their occupants to get out and walk or swim around. A scientist aboard a submarine like the Perry-Link *Deep Diver* can "park" the sub and leave it through a lockout chamber. With the submersible's powerful light to guide him, he can move a considerable distance away, making observations and gathering specimens.

Submersibles do not have to move to be useful to shelf explorers. Fixed-position underwater habitats, in which scientists can stay for days or weeks, do away with the need for divers to surface after each venture.

The *Hydrolab*, pictured here in its position on the sea floor, has been called "the first underwater classroom in the free world." Not the first in the world, because similar devices have been used by Soviet scientists.

In its first location, at a depth of 50 feet, one mile off Palm Beach, Florida, the *Hydrolab* was used by a succession of students and teachers from Florida Atlantic University. Divers can enter or leave it through a lockout chamber. It has a "dry" hatch into which a submersible can discharge passengers. The conning tower of the submersible comes up inside the hatch and locks into place. Passengers can then enter the *Hydrolab*, or leave it, without donning diving suits.

Much of the exploration of the continental shelf is carried out by scientists aboard surface ships. A variety of instruments are capable of penetrating the water and revealing the secrets of the sea floor. This small vessel, the *Eastward*, operated by Duke University's Marine Laboratory, is only 117.5 feet in length, with a beam of 28.5 feet, yet it has a capacity of 15 scientists and 15 crew members. In a series of voyages that crisscrossed an area of the sea off North Carolina, they used the *Eastward* to make the most intensive survey of any continental shelf area in the world.

When a violent storm lashed the North Pacific, scientists aboard this strange craft, called FLIP (for Floating Instrument Platform), were able to go right ahead with their investigation of the continental shelf off Alaska. Although angry waves, some 35 feet high, slammed against her steel sides, the craft hardly swayed.

What you're looking at in this photograph is only a small part of the craft, which is really 355 feet long. Some three hundred feet of that length are underwater. FLIP is towed to a site horizontally. When water is admitted to its ballast tanks, it "flips," the prow rising and the stern sinking. The six scientists and crewmen aboard have a secure platform from which to make observations.

Mapping land under the sea in detail was almost impossible before the development of today's electronic tools. One of the most important devices used in such detailed surveys of the continental shelf as that made from the *Eastward* is the echo sounder. Sound sent out from the ship bounces off the bottom and is reflected back to the ship, where it is picked up by a sensitive transducer (a type of microphone). The length of time it takes the echo to return determines the depth. Electronic apparatus records the depth readings from successive echoes as the ship moves slowly through the water. The result is a profile of the shelf area over which the ship has passed. This profile shows a submarine canyon.

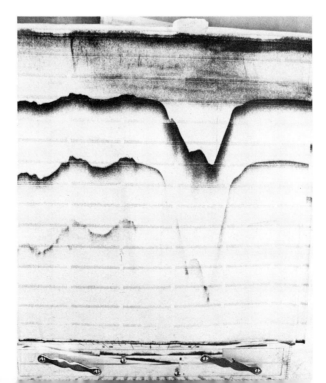

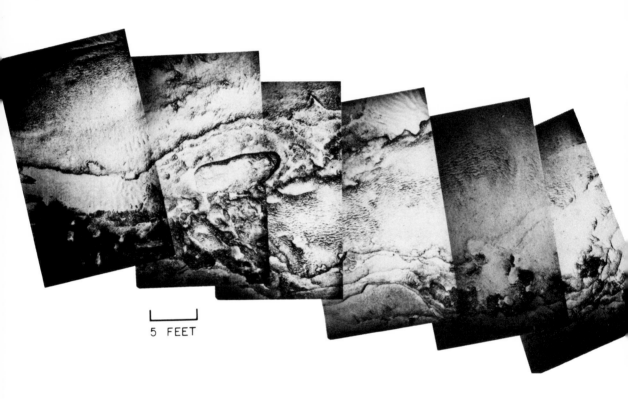

5 FEET

Cameras lowered from ships can produce remarkably detailed pictures of the water-covered land beneath.

Television cameras in special housings join with still cameras in providing a picture of what it's like on the continental shelf.

The search for geological and biological knowledge of the shelf does not stop with profiles and pictures. Revealing samples of material are brought up from the sea floor by a variety of grabs and dredges.

Some of the grabs, such as the one shown here, are called "clamshells" because they consist of two jaws which clamp shut after a spring is released when they hit bottom. Others are known as "orange peels" because their four jaws resemble an orange peel which has been cut into four longitudinal sections. Still another kind of grab is a steel box which scoops up samples as it is dragged along the sea floor.

Cameras are sometimes mounted right on the grabs so that scientists on the ship are given a good picture of just what the source of a given sample looks like.

The contents of any grab or dredge provide a fascinating range of specimens that tell much about the sea floor from which they came. These University of Maryland student biologists are examining clams.

What looks like a shell being studied by a U.S. Geological Survey scientist is really something quite different. It's the tooth of a mammoth, evidence that the continental shelf on which it was found was dry land not long ago in geological terms. Mammoths roved this now inundated region as recently as 11,000 years ago.

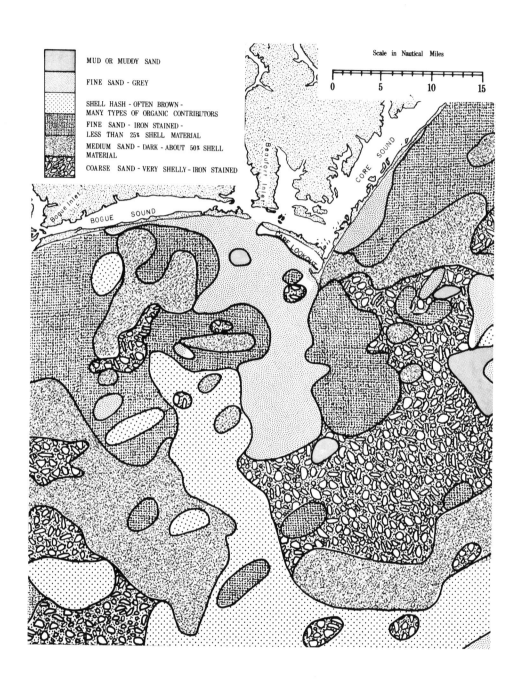

MUD OR MUDDY SAND

FINE SAND - GREY

SHELL HASH - OFTEN BROWN - MANY TYPES OF ORGANIC CONTRIBUTORS

FINE SAND - IRON STAINED - LESS THAN 25% SHELL MATERIAL

MEDIUM SAND - DARK - ABOUT 50% SHELL MATERIAL

COARSE SAND - VERY SHELLY - IRON STAINED

Scale in Nautical Miles

0   5   10   15

By using all the tools available, the explorers of the shelf are able to put together detailed maps showing the types of soil and sediment in any given area.

What's under the continental shelf? This is an important question the scientific explorers are seeking to answer. The knowledge they gain can tell them much about the geological history of the earth, and the treasure troves of oil and minerals that lie beneath submerged lands.

One way to discover underground secrets is to dig up actual samples of earth and rock. This is done with coring devices such as the one being dropped overside. When it plunges into the sea floor, a cylindrical sample of rock and soil is forced up inside the pipe. Some corers penetrate only a yard or so. Other kinds, which ingeniously use the pressure of sea water, can force their way down as much as sixty feet.

Samples of the soil extending hundreds or even thousands of feet under the continental shelf, or the floor of the deep sea beyond it, can be obtained by oil well drillers. No corers developed by ocean-ographers will go so deep, but the powerful diamond-studded drills that tap oil-bearing formations can be used to cut out samples. As in the simpler corers, these samples are forced into a pipe.

Laboratory examination enables geologists in laboratories aboard ship or on shore to read the messages of the cores. Sliced into sections, they are studied and analyzed. Their composition reveals the geological history of the continental shelf. To a skilled scientist it tells the story of the many changes of sea level, showing that the continental shelf has been both farther inland and farther out to sea than it is today. It tells what portions of the shelf were originally part of the main continent and which were created by sediment washing down from rivers. To the biologist and paleontologist, fossils found in the cores show what kind of dry land and marine life existed at any one time on what is now the continental shelf.

The vibrations created by explosions give scientists a way to "see" deep underground. Certain sharp sounds create a disturbance in the earth—a tiny manmade earthquake. Different types of soil and rock through which the shock waves pass cause them to be bent. As echoes from these waves come back to the ship or ships (often more than one is used in seismic sounding), a seismograph produces a record on paper that can be interpreted by geologists, like this University of Connecticut graduate student.

The sharp sounds needed for seismic soundings are easily created by explosives, but geologists have discovered that explosives used underwater disturb, and possibly damage, marine life. Environmentalists worried about the effects of thousands of explosive charges in the exploration of the shelf don't have to worry anymore. Engineers have developed a better, safer way to produce the sound. It's done with a "popper," a simple device in which a mixture of propane and oxygen is ignited by a spark plug inside a rubber sleeve. The sudden explosion is forceful enough to produce a strong seismic echo. Sea creatures even a few feet away are quite undisturbed.

2 · PROTECTING THE ENVIRONMENT OF THE CONTINENTAL SHELF

The concern shown on the faces of these biologists as they study the metabolism of marine organisms reflects the new attitude of science toward pollution of the continental shelves.

Until quite recently the waters along our coasts were looked upon as a perfectly safe place to dump garbage, sewage, and poisonous chemicals. Few people—not even most scientists—thought that these contaminants presented any danger to marine life. Now, as they study their effects on living creatures, ecologists know that we must face up to the problems of protecting the environment of the continental shelf. Its waters and floor are just as subject to the damaging effects of pollution as are our rivers, lakes, and soil.

This diver, who is examining a highly polluted portion of the continental shelf environment, is getting a firsthand look at the effects of dumping sewage into the sea. This outfall pipe near a Florida community has created a fouled area in which marine life has been destroyed by the buildup of waste.

In many other places along our shores, where communities send sewage into the supposedly accommodating waters of the "boundless ocean," conditions are equally bad. One of the major trouble spots along the Atlantic shelf is a few miles off the New Jersey coast. New York City annually transports some 4.5 million cubic yards of sludge from its sewage plants to this dumping ground, creating an area barren of all life. Studies show that the water above this place on the shelf contains only one part per million of oxygen. The minimum amount necessary to sustain life is 2.5 parts per million.

While pollution of the water by sewage has destructive effects on some marine organisms, it has the opposite effect on others. The sea urchins being studied by these Florida State University students are among those which are stimulated to abnormal growth by the nutrients found in sewage-polluted water. The result has been an enormous increase in the number of these creatures in some areas. These hordes of sea urchins, feeding on giant kelp, have virtually destroyed huge beds of this valuable seaweed off the California coast.

Scientists like Caltech's Dr. Wheeler North are studying ways to bring back the kelp. Divers have destroyed hundreds of thousands of the destructive sea urchins, but environmentalists are sure that the best way to stop such upsets in the balance of marine life is to stop dumping sewage on the shelf.

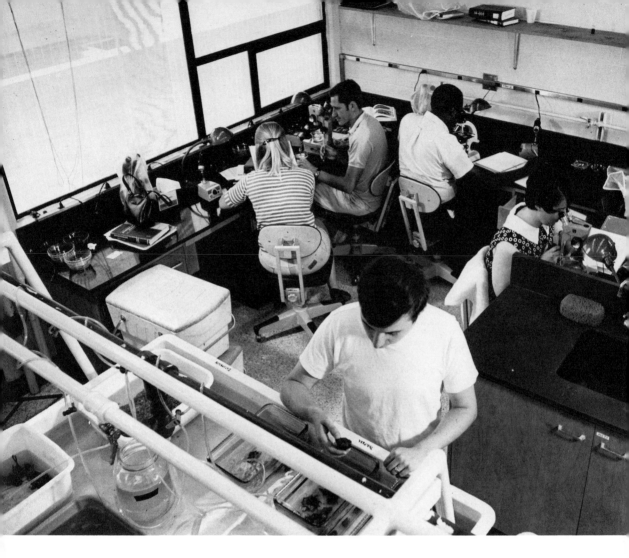

Chemicals poured out by factories menace not only marine organisms but human life as well. The problem is a serious one, for in the United States about 14,000 processing plants dump a half million different chemical compounds into the sea. In addition, DDT and other chemicals are washed into the sea by rivers.

The biological effects of these chemicals are not fully known, but many scientists and students, such as those shown here, in a Marine Science Center laboratory at Oregon State University, are investigating them.

One chemical, the dangers of which are well known, is mercury. Used by many industries, some one million pounds of it a year are dumped into shelf waters. Once in the sea water, it gets into the food cycle. Fish which eat small organisms that absorb mercury concentrate it in their tissues, although they themselves are not affected by it. If people eat fish containing high concentrates of mercury, they can be paralyzed or killed because mercury attacks the central nervous system of human beings. In the Japanese village of Minimata, some years ago, 105 people died from eating mercury-contaminated shellfish. No deaths have occurred in the United States, but alarming concentrations of mercury have been found in fish and other creatures.

Chemists are able to track down minute quantities of mercury by the use of an atomic absorption spectrometer, shown here. By measuring the vapor given off by mercury, it can detect amounts in water as low as one part in 10 billion.

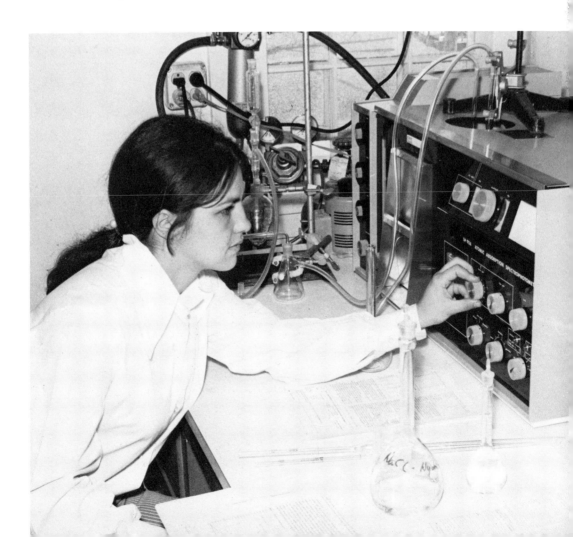

There is one pollutant which, although it endangers fish in rivers and lakes, may be safely emptied into shelf waters. When power plants which use water for cooling dump the heated water into a nearby stream, it often has a serious effect on aquatic life. A rise of 10° Fahrenheit in the water temperature doubles the amount of oxygen a fish needs to survive. Unfortunately, warmer water holds less oxygen, so that at the time it needs more the fish gets less. The result has been destruction of millions of fish near power plants.

Scientists have concluded that water which will dangerously raise the temperature of a river might safely be emptied into ocean water above the shelf. They are investigating the possibility that heated waste water could be channeled to the sea from power plants near the ocean. There it would actually be of benefit to fish farming operations. A slight rise in the temperature of water over an oyster bed, for instance, could greatly increase the yield of this seafood.

The biologist shown below is cleaning a net used in studying the effects of heated water on zooplankton.

The continental shelf can provide another dramatic solution to the hot water problem. Engineers propose that we get most of our electricity from nuclear power plants built on "power islands" in shallow waters along our coasts. These man-made islands could be built of earth and rocks dredged up from the shelves, as some, such as Island Esther in the Pacific, have been constructed to serve as platforms for oil wells.

The power plants on these islands would get their water from the sea, desalting it not only for cooling use, but to supply fresh water for water systems ashore. The hot water they return to the sea would either be harmlessly dissipated or used to serve nearby fish farms. Modern transmission systems would make it possible to send the electricity to cities far inland.

In one typical year, the U.S. Coast Guard, the government organization charged with standing guard against pollution of the waters above the continental shelf, investigated more than 1,000 cases of oil spills. Some came from offshore wells, some from damaged tankers, some from ships which deliberately dumped oil at sea.

Engineers are developing many ways to fight this menace to marine life and the beaches along our shores. Strict enforcement of safety measures can prevent most, if not all, of the disasters like the famous Santa Barbara oil spill, or the spectacular Gulf of Mexico oil well fire. If spills do occur, they can be kept from spreading by a variety of methods. One of them involves setting up a containment barrier made of plastic bags. Another uses machines which skim off the oil. Still another applies chemicals that "eat" up the oil.

To keep damaged tankers from disgorging their oil, the Coast Guard has devised an ingenious system for transferring the cargo to huge inflatable bags which could be dropped by parachute.

3 · DEVELOPING THE FOOD RESOURCES OF THE CONTINENTAL SHELF

To feed a hungry world, United Nations experts estimate, we must increase consumption of seafood at least ten times by the end of the century. Where will it all come from?

Much of it, with the aid of modern science, can be taken from the fertile waters above the continental shelves, particularly those off the United States and Canada. In fact, three-fourths of the world's present fish catch is made above the shelves of the Northern Hemisphere. A map showing the outlines of the continental shelves provides an almost exact outline of the richest fishing areas.

Although more fish naturally occur in these shallow waters, there just won't be enough to go around if catches are greatly increased. The problem for scientists engaged in "fisheries oceanography" is to find ways to produce far more fish than nature provides.

An exhaustive study of the food resources of the continental shelf is being made by many scientific organizations. These scientists, who are taking part in that study, are not catching fish to eat. Any halibut they haul in will be thrown back into the sea with a tag attached. A surprisingly large percentage of the fish they tag will be found again—perhaps as many as 60 percent. Some are caught by sports fishermen who respond to the request on the tag, asking the finder to mail it back. Others turn up in canneries, where they are spotted by alert workers. The places where the fish are found are often far from the places where they were tagged. By studying the distances travelled and the time elapsed fisheries oceanographers learn much about the habits of fish that make their homes in continental shelf waters.

Many ways to tag even tiny fish have been developed. One method is to use a simple heated marking tool that imprints a number indelibly on the side of the fish. This is most useful in marking small fish, like fingerling salmon, with code numbers that will enable scientists to identify the fish when they return to their spawning grounds. When it is desirable to have the tags returned, plastic strips or disks are attached to tail, fins, mouth, or gills.

Although the waters of the continental shelves abound in food resources, scientists are sure that, to meet the needs of the future, we must do more than accept nature's bounty. They are making plans to farm these waters, raising fish and other marine animals and plants. One step toward such aquaculture is the development of fish farms, areas where fish can be fed and readily "harvested."

How can fish be kept from just swimming away from fish farms where they are being raised? Some kind of fence in the sea may be necessary. It may be simply made of fish netting. It may consist of a curtain of air bubbles rising from a pipe laid along the bottom, or it can be an area of electrified water, through which fish are reluctant to swim.

Fishermen have often noticed concentrations of fish around sunken vessels. As an aid to fish farming, why not build homes for fish? This was a question asked some years ago by the underwater pioneer, Jacques Cousteau. He proposed the construction of "biatrons," concrete or plastic structures which would encourage the growth of fish colonies, making their care and harvesting easier. These concrete fish habitats, constructed on shore, are being lowered into California waters at the start of an experiment.

Other habitats provided for the fish in shallow California waters include old automobiles, piles of huge rocks, even an old-time streetcar.

Marine biologists making a detailed study of the more than 200 kinds of marine creatures which came to live in and around the structures, found that most fish preferred the "fish apartments." There, the number of fish was much greater than that around nearby natural reefs. An area of the continental shelf, which had previously had few fish in its waters, had been made productive by giving the fish a place to live.

Although it may be many years before working fish farms are actually operating, the California experiment, and many others like it, are proving that the shallow waters near our coasts can be used for aquaculture.

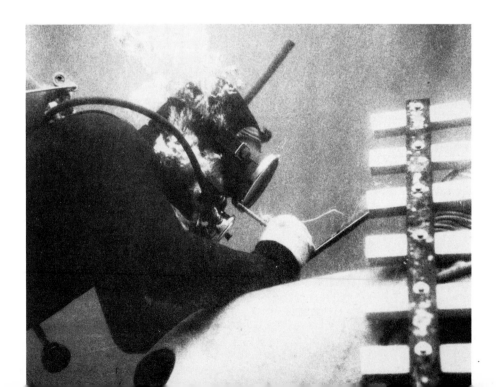

Another way to increase the fish yield of the shelf is to change the kind of fish that live there. On land, super meat animals have been bred. How about raising super fish? In scientific establishments on the Atlantic and Pacific coasts, many experiments in fish breeding are going on. Fish eggs are hatched in tanks where the water's temperature, salinity and nutritional content can be controlled.

Marine creatures other than fish may turn out to be the greatest food resource of the continental shelves. Aquaculturalists are exploring new ways to use the tremendous productive capacity of oysters. A single adult oyster lays as many as 500 million eggs in a season. Unfortunately, because many marine predators feed on oysters, only one in every 1,450,000 oysters ever reaches the age of three or four years required for it to be considered edible.

Scientists are seeking ways to keep predators out of oyster beds. Undersea fences and other marine growths that will discourage creatures which feed on oysters are two approaches. The most promising way to increase oyster crops, however, is to provide oysters with more "homes." The oyster larva spend the first hours of their lives seeking something to which they can attach themselves—a rock, a piece of wood, another oyster shell. Dumping broken oyster shells into the sea is the present method for encouraging oyster growth, but many experiments with plastic and wooden frameworks are being carried out.

Crabs, clams, scallops and lobsters are other edibles which may be used to increase the food yield of continental shelf waters. Many biologists are exploring the possibilities of farming such creatures, some kinds of which have not commonly been used for food.

The famous oceanographer Columbus O'Donnell Iselin, of Woods Hole Oceanographic Institution, once asserted that "90 percent of this rich food store" has been going to waste. The potential, if we turned to actively cultivating all the mollusks that might flourish on the shelf, he said, is "almost beyond calculation."

50

Seaweed grown as a food crop can greatly increase the nutritional resources of shallow waters near the coasts. There are many kinds of these aquatic plants, ranging from tiny ones that are almost microscopic, to giants more than 200 feet long.

Not all seaweed is good to eat, but many varieties are. Seaweed already goes into many common foods, such as ice cream and salad dressings, to which it helps impart a creamy consistency. In some parts of the world, it is commonly eaten as a salad and as a cooked vegetable. Nutritionists have been experimenting with grinding up seaweed to make a flour which can be mixed with wheat flour in the baking of breads, cookies, and cakes, adding to their food value.

Seaweed is already cultivated along the continental shelves of both the Atlantic and the Pacific, where scientists are working to find and develop the kind of seaweed which will grow best as commercial crops. They are also trying to find ways of harvesting seaweed that will be more efficient than the present method of raking it in from small boats. Soon harvesting machines may be moving across watery seaweed fields.

Any study of the food potential of continental shelf waters calls for considering plankton, the masses of tiny plants and animals that float in certain parts of the sea. Plankton is at the start of the ocean's food chain. Small fish eat the plankton, larger fish eat these fish, and still larger fish eat them.

Increasing the quantity of plankton in fish-raising areas could increase the number of fish that could be raised there. Growth of plankton could be encouraged by warming the water, and by pumping water up from lower levels, where the minute plants and animals abound, to the levels nearer the surface, where fish customarily swim.

Some scientists ask whether we should go to the bother of raising fish at all. It takes 10 pounds of plankton to produce one pound of edible fish. Why not simply eat the plankton, they ask, increasing the yield of food as much as ten times? This "soup of the sea" could be made into protein-rich flour that could be mixed with other foods. The problem lies in straining it out of the water. One scientist estimates that it would be necessary to screen a volume of water 60 times larger than an average school classroom to get the protein equivalent of a pound of beans.

The large plankton net drawn behind a ship in an experiment sponsored by the National Marine Fisheries Service is one way of gathering plankton in quantity. The marine biologist collecting plankton in a small hand net will study it later in a laboratory. If plankton can be utilized for food, it could greatly increase the protein productivity of the continental shelf. Efforts like these are the kind of experiments that will prove whether the dream of commonly-eaten "planktonburgers" can be made a practical reality.

4 · DEVELOPING THE MINERAL RESOURCES OF THE CONTINENTAL SHELF

In the past 30 years the world has used more minerals than it did in all its history up to that time. In the next 30 years we will use up the earth's mineral resources at an even greater rate as the requirements of developing nations increase and our own needs in the United States continue to climb.

Can we find enough new mineral deposits to meet these growing needs? That is a question many authorities are asking. Fortunately, as resources of the "dry continents" dwindle, we are learning about the immense possibilities of the continental shelves and the ocean depths.

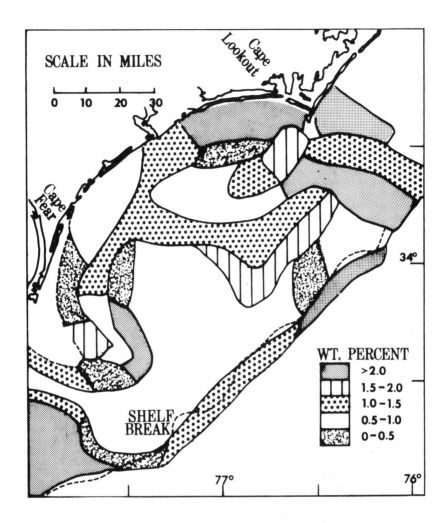

SCALE IN MILES

0 10 20 30

Cape Lookout

Cape Fear

34°

WT. PERCENT

>2.0
1.5–2.0
1.0–1.5
0.5–1.0
0–0.5

SHELF BREAK

77°   76°

Explorations now going on, by methods which range from shipborne instruments to searches by diving geologists, lead to estimates that at least 500,000 square miles of the North American shelves are "mineralized." Not much of this huge area has yet been explored, but many important mineral discoveries have already been made, including gold on the shelf off Alaska, platinum-bearing sand off the state of Washington, and titanium off Florida.

A map of one intensively studied area, off the coast of North Carolina, gives a hint of just how much mineral wealth may be concealed beneath the shelf. The figures shown on the map are percentages, in weight, of heavy metals.

How will these underwater riches be mined and brought to the surface? Mining engineers propose a variety of methods. In very shallow water, dredges let down from ships will be the simplest devices. They can simply scrape along the bottom and, when full, be hoisted to the ship. Another way calls for seagoing "vacuum cleaners," pipes that would suck ores up into the holds of ships. A third scheme would connect close-to-shore mines with the mainland by tunnels.

The boldest plans envision a whole new breed of submersible machinery engaging in open pit mining, with huge mechanical shovels loading the ore into submarine trucks.

No digging will be required to get at one kind of mineral treasure found on the floor of both the continental shelf and the ocean-covered land beyond it. Huge quantities of the strange black rocks called manganese nodules lie on the sandy floor, waiting to be scooped up. Manganese is not the only mineral in them. They are also rich in nickel, copper and cobalt, and contain some cadmium, zinc, molybdenum, vanadium, and many other elements.

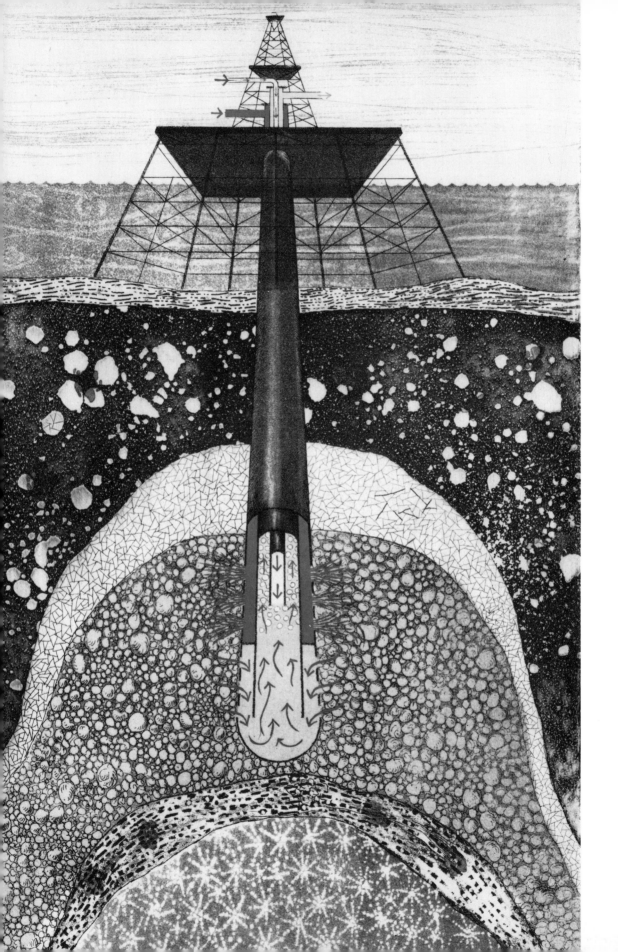

Sulfur, the golden substance called "brimstone" in the Bible, is a vital material in our modern world. It goes into fertilizers and is used in many chemical processes by the papermaking industry and others. It is another mineral that presents no mining problems, and deposits of it found on the continental shelf are already being extracted.

In this pioneering sulfur mine, seven miles off Louisiana, the sulfur-bearing formation is pierced by a series of drill holes into which pipes are inserted. Steam is forced down the pipes, heating the rock and causing the sulfur to melt. It can then be pumped to the platform as a liquid which will later solidify.

When they run wild, offshore oil wells menace the environment with black smudges of oil that ruin beaches and endanger marine and bird life. However, even the most concerned environmentalists agree that in a world running short of oil we must tap the great oil reservoirs on the continental shelves. Natural gas also exists in huge quantities under the shelves. This is fortunate, because shortages of this clean-burning fuel, which aids our fight on air pollution, make it urgent that we find new supplies.

Geologists estimate that oil and natural gas on the shelves are abundant enough to meet as much as half our needs for these vital fuels.

The greatest mineral riches of the continental shelf may someday come from the water that covers it. Analyses of sea water samples show that it contains 60 of the 92 natural elements, including a wealth of minerals useful to man. Scientists calculate that in every cubic mile of sea water, suspended in the form of particles invisible to the naked eye, are these amounts of valuable minerals:

Sodium chloride (common salt)	128 million tons
Magnesium chloride	18 million tons
Magnesium sulphate	8 million tons
Calcium sulphate	6 million tons
Potassium sulphate	4 million tons
Calcium carbonate (lime)	578 thousand tons
Magnesium bromide	350 thousand tons
Bromine	300 thousand tons
Strontium	60 thousand tons
Boron	21 thousand tons
Barium	900 tons
Iodine	700 tons
Arsenic	250 tons
Rubidium	200 tons
Silver	40 tons
Copper, lead, zinc, magnesium	30 tons
Gold	25 tons
Uranium	7 tons

The engineering problems that must be overcome before any of this mineral wealth can be extracted are formidable. Getting out the salt is simple. Man has done that for centuries by simply letting the water evaporate from ponds by the sea, leaving the salt behind. The difficulty in extracting other substances from sea water lies in the high cost of straining vast quantities of it. Magnesium and bromine have been extracted successfully, but engineers are still baffled by other minerals. To capture the elusive gold in sea water, for instance, it would be necessary to process one million gallons of water to get .005 ounce of the precious metal. Finding ways to make sea water yield its fabulous wealth remains a challenge for engineers of the future to solve.

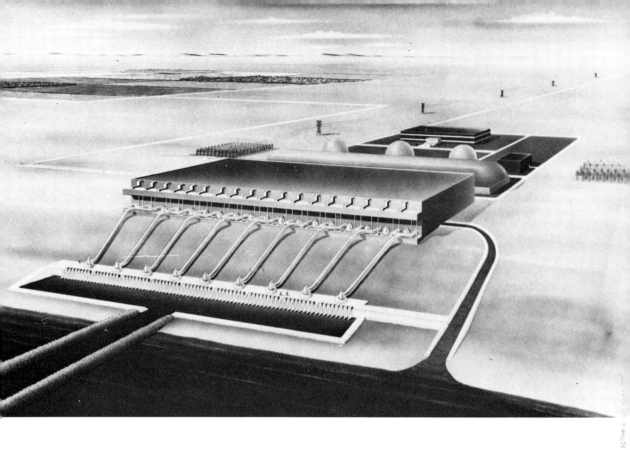

Water systems which get their water from lakes, streams, and deep wells are having a hard time keeping up with the demands of an industrialized world. It takes over 350,000 gallons of water to make a ton of rayon; a million gallons of water to produce 1,000 gallons of gasoline. If you're an average water user, you use 200 gallons a day in your home for all domestic purposes—a total of almost 75,000 gallons a year.

Today, engineers are coming close to realizing the old dream of finding an economical way to turn salt water into fresh water. Built on the shore, or on man-made islands in the shallow waters above the shelves, atomic plants like the one shown in the artist's conception can provide both water and electricity. This plant, much larger than any experimental ones in operation today, is designed to desalt a billion gallons of sea water a day.

5 · WORKING ON THE CONTINENTAL SHELF

"The experiments in underwater living and working that are already successfully going on open vistas of farming, oil drilling, and mining, and otherwise using the continental shelves by working *down there* instead of, as we now do, with our tools suspended on the end of a string from the wobbly surface of a ship."

This statement by Dr. Athelstan Spilhaus, director of the Franklin Institute, indicates the possibility that thousands of workers may someday have jobs right on the continental shelf. Pipelines, cables, underwater power plants, laboratories, even underwater cities will provide a variety of opportunities for men and women who want to work on a new frontier.

To help them carry out their work, all kinds of new equipment will be available. Much of the activity will call for diving with improved forms of scuba, such as this rebreather apparatus being tried out by a woman scientist. It is lighter than traditional scuba gear calling for twin tanks and, most important, it enables a diver to stay down for up to 12 hours at a stretch.

A variety of propulsion units, such as this sea sled, will carry workers quickly from one location to another.

Some of the jobs on the shelf will be carried out by workers aboard submarines equipped with mechanical arms that can imitate human movements. Run from a control board, they will enable the operator to perform many tasks, such as positioning markers, gathering geological specimens, and moving equipment.

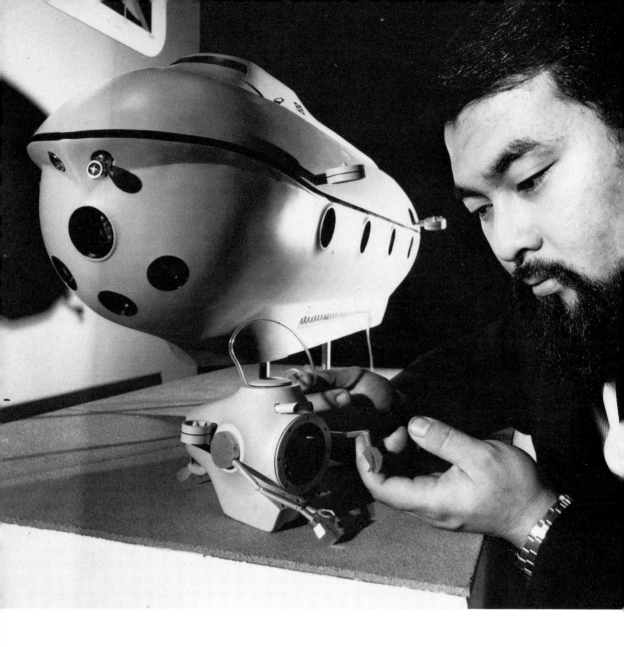

This model of a submersible for use on the shelf and the deep ocean floor was designed by students at California State College at Long Beach. The system consists of a mother vehicle with dependent work pods. The mother vehicle, powered by fuel cells, contains the power and life support systems that extend the usefulness of the pods, which are detachable from the ship. Umbilical cords that stay attached to the mother ship provide the pods with power for lights and actuating the mechanical arms as they move about.

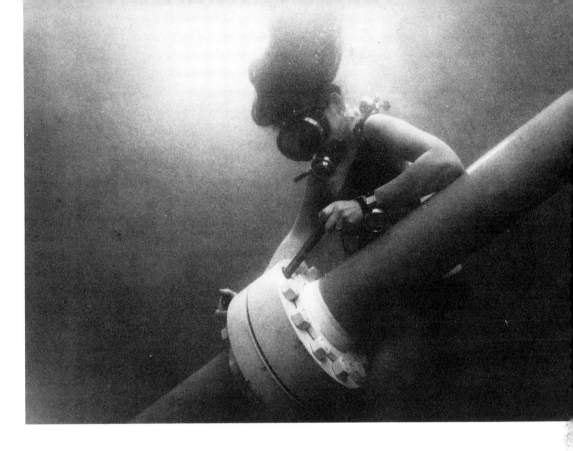

Many kinds of tools that will operate underwater will be used in carrying out shelf jobs. Power wrenches, saws, and even welding equipment are being adapted. They must be made easier to handle than tools for use in the atmosphere. Learning to use them takes long practice by undersea workers.

Some shelf workers will be assisted by porpoises which have been trained to carry out many tasks for their human masters. Porpoises and dolphins, rated as possibly the most intelligent of all animals, have already demonstrated their ability to serve man. They can carry tools, deliver messages written on slates from one diver to another,

and locate lost equipment dropped by a worker.

These porpoises, trained by Navy divers, are highly skilled. One is shown tripping a buzzer on a ship to indicate that he has come back from carrying out a mission. The other is completing delivery of an instrument package to a diver.

Work connected with power plants will provide many jobs on the continental shelf. The many permanent installations, such as under-sea laboratories, will need electricity, as will fish farms, mines, and oil pumping stations. Some will be supplied by electricity from power islands on the surface.

Underwater power plants, such as an experimental one being installed in 150 feet of water off California, will probably be most widely used. This miniature power plant, which could be a prototype for much larger ones, gets its power from radioisotopes. As they decay they give off heat which is converted to electricity.

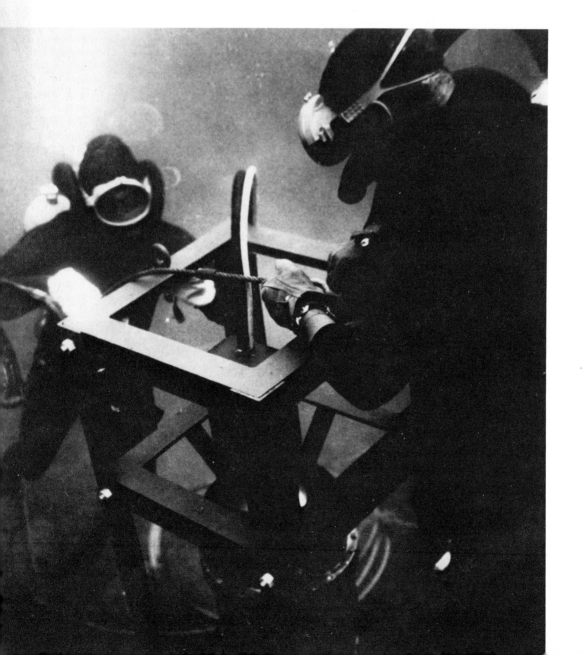

With abundant power, the shelf can be used for many kinds of oil operations. This artist's conception of a future undersea oil field includes a complete refinery, oil storage tanks, and workers' homes (the smaller domes near the storage tanks). The inflated buoyancy bags at the left support the pipes that bring up oil from wells underneath.

Submarine tankers like those shown in the lower photo could pull long trains of inflatable oil tanks.

Many workers on the new American continent will be engaged in salvage operations, for the shelf is a graveyard of ships. You can get some idea of the salvage possibilities by looking at a part of a wreck map showing some of the ships that have gone down off the North Carolina coast. Each of the numbers indicates the location of a known shipwreck. In the past 400 years, more than 2,000 ships have met a watery end on the shelf off Cape Hatteras.

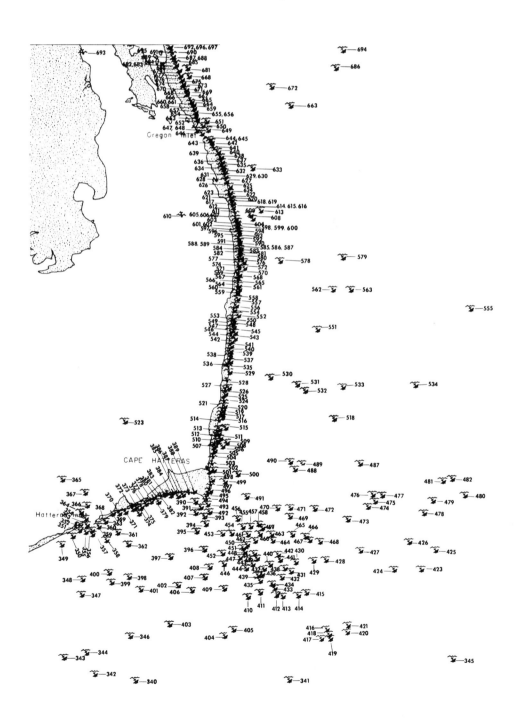

Many of the ships that will be the targets of salvagers are not of much value. Others could yield fabulous returns. One known ship, for example, was loaded with 10,000 tons of tin concentrate which would be worth $26 million if it could be brought to the surface.

As workers move onto the shelf, many new methods of salvage are being devised. One promising method is to use air-filled buoyancy tanks which, attached to the hull of a sunken vessel, could exert enough force to lift the ship from its resting place.

Many workers on the shelf may be employed on projects which could help ease the water shortages that confront some American cities—the building of immense aqueducts to carry water from areas where it is plentiful to regions where it is scarce. For instance, one could run from the Pacific Northwest, which has surplus water, to southern California, which is short of it.

Schemes to convey water long distances are not new, but the idea of putting an aqueduct on the shelf is. Engineers see many advantages to locating it there. It would be much easier to lay a huge pipe along the sea floor than it would be to run it overland or to dig canals. There would be no problems of disfiguring the landscape and disrupting the streets and buildings of congested urban areas.

Giant pipes, more than 30 feet in diameter, could be floated to their sites and then sunk into place. Once anchored they would be secure from storms which might lash the surface. Made of non-corrosive materials, they would require little maintenance. They would not harm the environment of the shelf in any way. In fact, by serving as artificial reefs, they would increase the number of fish living in shelf waters.

Mending the nets that may be used to keep fish within the waters of undersea farms will be only one of the many tasks that will be assigned to workers on the shelf. When the continental shelves are fully used to produce the seafood needed by a hungry world there will be work for biologists, engineers, and technicians.

6 · PLAYING ON THE CONTINENTAL SHELF

The surface of the water above the continental shelf has long been a playground for swimmers, boaters, surfers, and fishermen.

Now hundreds of thousands of people seek recreation *in* the water and on the land floor beneath. Tomorrow, their number will increase to millions.

Skin divers can enjoy the aquatic wonderland of the continental shelf with no more equipment than flippers and a simple face plate. A lot of looking can be done in the 30 to 60 seconds that a diver can hold his breath.

Add a snorkel—a simple tube that reaches above the water to deliver air from the surface—and the stay in shallow water can be extended indefinitely.

The real key that unlocks all the visual treasures of the shelf is scuba. (The letters stand for Self-Contained Underwater Breathing Apparatus.) The apparatus consists of three main parts—a tank or tanks containing compressed air; a regulator which reduces the pressure of the air to correspond with the diver's depth, and times the release of air to fit the diver's needs; and a mouthpiece and hose connected to the regulator. At a depth of 30 feet a diver can stay down for about an hour on a tankful of air.

What do you do when you get down there? You may choose just to look, but you may regard your venture into shelf waters as an opportunity to add a new realm to amateur photography. Photos of fish, ocean plants, odd geological formations, or fellow divers all make good subjects. This photographer is taking pictures of staghorn coral on the shelf near Marathon, Florida.

While cameras used by professionals are expensive, ordinary low-priced cameras can be mounted in waterproof housings costing less than $25. Near the surface, enough sunlight for picture-taking filters down. For shots in deeper water, photographers use flash attachments.

The shelf provides abundant opportunities for a variety of hobbies. Collecting specimens—such as the starfish-like sand dollar being carefully dug out of the sand by a skin diver—is just one of them. Amateur geologists, botanists, and zoologists all find fascinating prizes in the shallow waters along our coasts.

Many amateur scientists are making contributions to oceanographic knowledge by their activities. Members of the American Littoral Society, a band of amateur divers, have aided biologists in many projects involving the study of fish on natural and artificial reefs. In one experiment they tagged hundreds of fish off New England. In another they studied the growth of reef life near a sunken freighter off New Jersey. On the coast off California amateur scientists aided in an attack on sea urchins, which were damaging the seaweed crop. The 800 scuba divers who participated in the drive destroyed almost a million sea urchins.

Other amateur undersea scientists are helping to improve living conditions for fish on the shelf. Old tires make excellent artificial reefs. Once they are in place, they last indefinitely. A number of tires can be fastened together with metal rods to provide larger habitats, or they can be dropped into the water one at a time. They are unsightly in junk yards, where they pile up by the millions, but on the shelf old tires quickly become covered with sediment and marine growth that makes them blend with their surroundings. The important thing is—fish like them!

The U.S. Park Service has 47 National Parks, Monuments, Seashores, and Historical Sites in coastal locations. Not all of them have underwater recreation areas, but many do. In addition, many states have underwater parks or are planning to develop them.

Many of these facilities will have marked trails with scuba-diving park naturalists serving as combined lifeguards and guides to natural wonders.

7 · LIVING ON THE NEW AMERICAN CONTINENT

A home on the continental shelf? This once might have seemed like a wild dream, but experiments in underwater living have shown that human beings can live comfortably for long periods of time in underwater habitats.

In the *Sealab II* experiments, three teams of aquanauts lived under 195 feet of water off La Jolla, California. Their tanklike habitat was placed in a location which was considered "typical of continental shelf conditions." The three teams, totalling 28 men, stayed underwater a total of 45 days in an effort to prove that in suitable quarters people can live for considerable lengths of time under any conditions that would be found anywhere on the continental shelf of the United States. "To work on the shelf we must learn to *live* on the shelf," said Commander Scott Carpenter, the astronaut turned aquanaut who was a team leader in *Sealab II*. Dramatic documentation of this came when it was found that one diver, living underwater, could do as much work in a six-hour period as thirty-five divers operating from the surface.

Sealab aquanauts had all the comforts of home, including hot meals. They never had any reason to feel out of touch with the world because they were in telephone communication, not only with people on dry land, but with the inhabitants of another underwater dwelling, *Conshelf III*. This habitat, developed by Jacques Cousteau, was positioned on the continental shelf off Europe, 6,000 miles away from *Sealab*.

Another pioneering experiment in underwater living was called *Tektite*. In a completely equipped habitat under 50 feet of water in Lameshur Bay, the Virgin Islands, four scientists lived for two months without coming to the surface. In a later experiment, *Tektite II*, a series of stays was made by eleven teams, each consisting of four scientists and an engineer. Each team occupied *Tektite* for two to three weeks while carrying out some important underwater mission such as studying marine life, sea floor geology, and human physiology in underwater situations.

One team was made up wholly of women scientists, one of whom is shown here relaxing in the control room of *Tektite*.

Making full use of their 24-hours-a-day life underwater, the research teams spent much of their time outside their *Tektite* quarters. Their ventures into the aquatic world around them were made at various times of the day and night.

One member of the women's team, Sylvia Earl, wrote that they "came to know individual plants, fishes, queen conches, lobsters, starfishes and others. . . . Animals took little notice of our presence . . . within a short time we came to regard ourselves, and perhaps to be regarded, as members of the reef community."

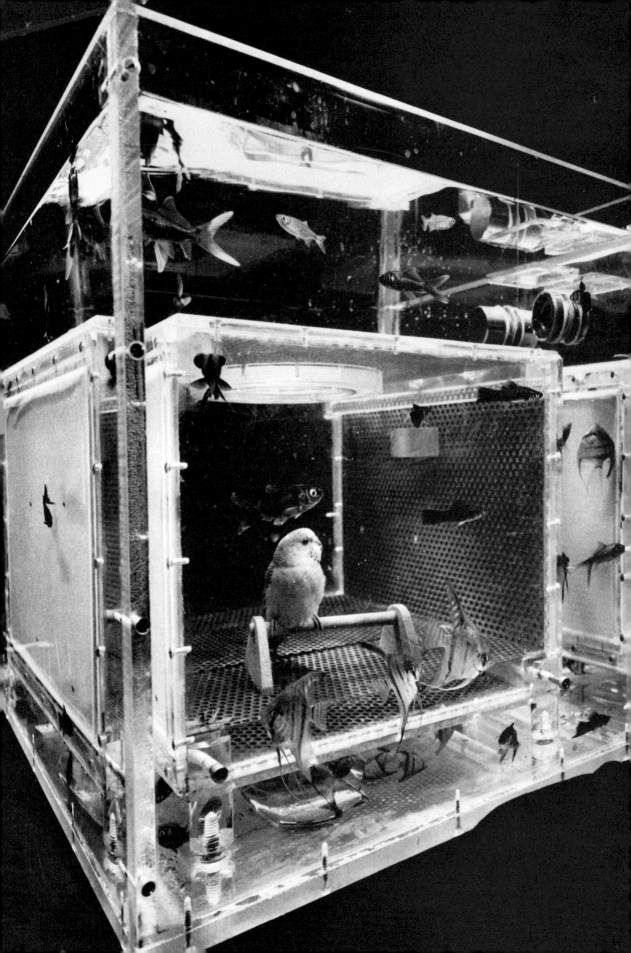

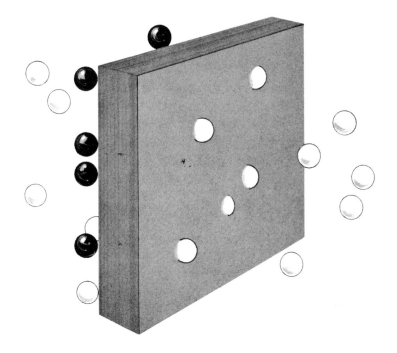

Providing air for people living in shelf dwellings is a problem for which scientists may have found a startling answer. They say we can simply extract oxygen from the water surrounding the sea floor structures. All the oxygen this parrot is breathing comes from the water surrounding his cage.

What makes this possible is the use of special plastic membranes. They exclude all water molecules, but admit oxygen molecules through tiny openings. (In the diagram the white spheres represent the oxygen molecules.) The action of the molecules is based on a law of physics, known as "the partial pressure of gases," which states that molecules of a gas will move to an adjacent area where there is a lesser supply of the gas.

In an underwater structure this would work by having a chamber in which sea water flowed against banks of membranes. The oxygen extracted from the water would be distributed through the structure by an air-conditioning system.

The same law would be put to work to purify the air. Carbon dioxide exhaled by the dwellers in the structure would be distributed into the sea water by other membranes. This process is also going on in the case of the parrot in the tank.

Designers propose many types of structures that would permit living on the continental shelf. One of them is a series of spheres which could be joined together in any number of multiples. They could be used for living quarters, offices or laboratories. Some would have smaller, all-glass spheres attached to them to permit observation of marine life.

Someday you may spend a weekend at a hotel on the continental shelf. This design for such a hotel was developed by student industrial designers at California State College at Long Beach. The underwater resort would offer accommodations for 1,500 people. Decks are above water, the rooms for guests underwater, with the "ground floor" rooms on the shelf itself.

Prophets of the future even predict that individual homes may be set up on the shelf. Made of plastic, concrete, or light rustproof metal, they could be assembled on the surface and transported to their sites on the sea floor by submarine tugs and tractors. Many people, instead of having a second home at a lake, the seashore, or in the mountains, might choose to have a vacation home on the new American continent.

GOVERNMENTAL SOURCES OF INFORMATION ABOUT THE CONTINENTAL SHELF

Atomic Energy Commission
Washington, D.C. 20545

Bureau of Mines
Washington, D.C. 20240

Bureau of Reclamation
Washington, D.C. 20240

Coast Guard
400 Seventh St., S.W.
Washington, D.C. 20591

Environmental Protection Agency
401 M St., S.W.
Washington, D.C. 20024

Geological Survey
Washington, D.C. 20242

National Academy of Sciences
2101 Constitution Ave.
Washington, D.C. 20418

National Aeronautics and
Space Administration
Washington, D.C. 20546

National Marine Fisheries Service
Interior Building
Washington, D.C. 20235

National Oceanic and
Atmospheric Administration
Washington, D.C. 20230

National Park Service
Washington, D.C. 20240

Naval Research Laboratory
4555 Overlook Ave., S.W.
Washington, D.C. 20390

Office of the Oceanographer
of the Navy
732 N. Washington St.
Alexandria, Va. 22314

Office of Naval Research
800 N. Quincy St.
Arlington, Va. 22217

Office of Saline Water
18th and C Sts., N.W.
Washington, D.C. 20240

Office of Water Resources Research
19th and C Sts., N.W.
Washington, D.C. 20240

Smithsonian Institution
Office of Oceanography
and Limnology
Washington, D.C. 20560

SUGGESTIONS FOR FURTHER READING

Although there is a lack of popular books about the continental shelf, much information about it is to be found in books about the oceans and oceanography. The following are recommended:

Caidín, Martin, *Hydrospace*. New York, Dutton, 1964.

Carson, Rachel, *The Sea Around Us*. New York, Oxford, 1961.

Gaskell, T.F., *World Beneath the Oceans*. Garden City, Doubleday.

Idyll, C.P., *The Sea Against Hunger*. New York, Crowell, 1970.

Lee, Owen, *The Skin Diver's Bible*. Garden City, Doubleday.

Marx, Wesley, *The Frail Ocean*. New York, Coward, 1970.

Michelsohn, David Reuben, *The Oceans in Tomorrow's World*. New York, Messner, 1972.

Millard, Reed, *Clean Air—Clean Water for Tomorrow's World*. New York, Messner, 1971.

North, Wheeler J., *The Golden Guide to Scuba Diving*. New York, Golden Press, 1968.

Soule, Gardner, *Wide Oceans*. New York, Rand, 1970.

INDEX

ABOUT THE AUTHOR

Norman Carlisle, editorial director of Science Book Associates, is an editor, writer, and audiovisual specialist in the field of career guidance. As a writer, he is the author or co-author of more than five hundred articles appearing in national publications. While he has been active in reporting on a variety of scientific developments, he is particularly concerned with those that affect our environment. He makes his home in New Mexico but is a frequent visitor to the oceans that lap our continent. His abiding interest in them is reflected in this exploration of THE NEW AMERICAN CONTINENT.